BOO! Thirteen Scenes From Halloween

by
PAT COOK

Dramatic Publishing
Woodstock, Illinois • London, England • Melbourne, Australia

*** NOTICE ***

The amateur and stock acting rights to this work are controlled exclusively by THE DRAMATIC PUBLISHING COMPANY without whose permission in writing no performance of it may be given. Royalty fees are given in our current catalogue and are subject to change without notice. Royalty must be paid every time a play is performed whether or not it is presented for profit and whether or not admission is charged. A play is performed anytime it is acted before an audience. All inquiries concerning amateur and stock rights should be addressed to:

DRAMATIC PUBLISHING
P. O. Box 129, Woodstock, Illinois 60098.

COPYRIGHT LAW GIVES THE AUTHOR OR THE AUTHOR'S AGENT THE EXCLUSIVE RIGHT TO MAKE COPIES. This law provides authors with a fair return for their creative efforts. Authors earn their living from the royalties they receive from book sales and from the performance of their work. Conscientious observance of copyright law is not only ethical, it encourages authors to continue their creative work. This work is fully protected by copyright. No alterations, deletions or substitutions may be made in the work without the prior written consent of the publisher. No part of this work may be reproduced or transmitted in any form or by any means, electronic or mechanical, including photocopy, recording, videotape, film, or any information storage and retrieval system, without permission in writing from the publisher. It may not be performed either by professionals or amateurs without payment of royalty. All rights, including but not limited to the professional, motion picture, radio, television, videotape, foreign language, tabloid, recitation, lecturing, publication, and reading are reserved. *On all programs this notice should appear:*

"Produced by special arrangement with
THE DRAMATIC PUBLISHING COMPANY of Woodstock, Illinois"

©MCMXCIV by
PAT COOK

Printed in the United States of America
All Rights Reserved
(BOO! THIRTEEN SCENES FROM HALLOWEEN)

Cover design by Susan Carle

ISBN 0-87129-436-2

BOO! Thirteen Scenes From Halloween

For a Flexible Cast
(As few as 5 for 38 parts)

TABLE OF CONTENTS

<u>ACT ONE</u>
Knock Knock 7
Curse Of The Ugly Dolls 11
I Hate Halloween 16
Out For Blood 19
A Little Blackmail 20
The Perfect Mask 24
Two Heads Are Better Than One 26
A Very Dirty Trick 29
A Very Sweet Treat 33
This'll Scare You To Death 35
Grave Situation 40
Better Late Than Never 44

<u>ACT TWO</u>
Her Last Possession 49

AUTHOR'S NOTE

BOO! is a group of sketches with a decidedly sinister tone. They deal with both the misunderstood of the daylight and the fearsome of the night. Each calls for skeletal (what else) sets and a minimum of costume changes, sometimes no more than a change of mask. An emcee may be added to introduce each story. He or she may even be something of a "character," along the lines of Boris Karloff or Rod Serling or Elvira.

This Halloween review can be produced utilizing two areas of a stage, alternating main stage with the apron or stage left with stage right, indicating beginning and ends of the vignettes with light cues. The final story In Act Two, "Her Last Possession," requires more of a legitimate set, which is drawn out at the beginning of the act. The rest of these stories vary in length, some short plays, some only blackouts, and each with a decided twist at the end.

ACT ONE

Knock Knock

Characters: LYDIA, CHARLEY

(The setting includes two doors—one, located L, leads to the kitchen and the other, R, leads to the outside. Two chairs are situated DL, with a table between them. CHARLEY is reading a newspaper in one chair and his wife, LYDIA, sits quietly in the other. She looks at CHARLEY and almost giggles. Finally, she can contain herself no longer.)

LYDIA. Knock knock.
CHARLEY. Lydia, I'm reading the paper.
LYDIA. Knock knock.
CHARLEY *(disgustedly)*. Who's there?
LYDIA. Vampire.
CHARLEY. Vampire who?
LYDIA. What, you're just going to open the door for a vampire? *(CHARLEY jumps up and throws his newspaper on the floor.)*
CHARLEY. You did it again! You do this to me every time. I'm sick of it!
LYDIA. Sick of what?
CHARLEY. Your stupid knock knock jokes!
LYDIA. You used to *like* my jokes.
CHARLEY. That's back when. WAAAAY back when.
LYDIA. When when?
CHARLEY. What?
LYDIA. When when?

CHARLEY. That sounds like knock knock!

LYDIA. Back when did you like my jokes?

CHARLEY *(pacing)*. Back when you had a sense of humor. Back when you had some variety in your conversation. Back when you had a little wit about you. Not just the same old thing over and over. You used to tell wonderful stories. You used puns, you came up with riddles. Every once in awhile you'd give me a sob story or a shaggy dog story. A little head humor every now and then. Even limericks! Remember those?

LYDIA. I'm sorry.

CHARLEY *(grabs his newspaper)*. Yeah, sure. *(He resumes his chair and begins reading again.)*

LYDIA. I didn't know it bothered you so much.

CHARLEY. Mmmmbmbmgmmm.

LYDIA. Okay. Okay, you want a limerick. Here's a limerick. *(CHARLEY lowers his paper and looks at her.)*
   A lady of wellborn stock
   Caused her husband to go into shock
   At the clinic they say
   Found the husband that way
   'Cause his wife always said "Knock knock"!

CHARLEY *(throws down the newspaper and jumps up)*. AHHHHH! *(LYDIA covers her mouth with her hand to keep him from seeing her laugh.)* Oh. I get it. That's your plan, is it? That's what all this is about, isn't it?

LYDIA. What?

CHARLEY. The clinic, the nuthouse. That's your little plan, isn't it? Drive old Charley's brain into bubble gum and you're rid of me. That's it, isn't it?

LYDIA. Hon, some wives don't talk to their husbands at all.

CHARLEY *(laughing maniacally)*. Who? Find out if they teach a course.

LYDIA. All this fuss over such a little thing.

CHARLEY. Yeah?

LYDIA. Yes.

CHARLEY. Bacteria's a little thing and a lot of people die from it!

LYDIA. Charley, you need to relax.

CHARLEY *(grabs his newspaper)*. Don't tell me to relax. I'm fine. You don't need to worry about old Charley 'cause he's on to you. *(He sits.)* And I'm perfectly relaxed. *(He flexes the newspaper and tears it in half.)* I was through with that, anyway.

LYDIA. Oh, Charley, you...you don't love me anymore! *(She begins sobbing and takes a handkerchief from her apron, weeping into it.)*

CHARLEY. No! Wait. *(He softens a bit.)* Look, I didn't mean anything by it.

LYDIA. I mean, don't you think I had a reason to tell you my knock knock jokes? They build up to a punch line. Something unexpected.

CHARLEY. Yeah, I know, I...*(He moves toward her.)*

LYDIA. They're for a reason, I'm not just trying to drive you nuts! They're building up to the unexpected punch, but NO! You can't wait, you have to...to...scream at me and...and...*(Crying uncontrollably, she rushes out the kitchen door.)*

CHARLEY. Lydia! Lydia? I'm sorry. Hon? Look, I won't scream anymore. I promise.

LYDIA *(offstage)*. Yes, you will! You don't love me anymore!

CHARLEY. Yes, I do. I must to put up with this. Hon? Look. *(He sits in his chair again.)* I'm sitting down and I'm not upset anymore. Lydia? Please come out. I just had a bad day today. I tell you what. I'll just sit here and we'll pretend nothing has happened and you...*(He winces.)*...you can tell your little joke all over again. Okay?

(LYDIA enters, her face still covered with her handkerchief.)

LYDIA. You promise?
CHARLEY. Go ahead. *(He smiles broadly.)* See? I'm not expecting anything. Go ahead. Knock knock.
LYDIA. Knock knock.
CHARLEY. Who's there? *(LYDIA moves up behind him.)*
LYDIA. Vampire.
CHARLEY. Vampire who? *(LYDIA takes down the handkerchief to reveal she now has two very prominent canine teeth.)*
LYDIA. What, you're just going to open the door for a vampire! AAAHHH! *(She leans over quickly and bites CHARLEY on the neck while he screams.)*

BLACKOUT

Curse Of The Ugly Dolls

Characters: MARSHA, MAXINE, BETTY

(Lights come up to find three girls, dressed in their robes, sitting on the floor. BETTY and MAXINE are each holding a pillow and staring wide-eyed at MARSHA as she finishes a story.)

MARSHA. ...so then the wife took down her handkerchief and she had these two long teeth sticking out of her mouth and she says, "What, you're just going to open the door for a vampire?" And she jumps on him and...! *(At the word "jumps" the other two girls squeal and hide their face in their pillow.)*
MAXINE. Oh, that's just so stupid.
MARSHA. Was not.
MAXINE. Was too.
MARSHA. You jumped!
BETTY. Yeah, you jumped. You're the one that's stupid.
MAXINE. Nah ah.
BETTY. Uh huh.
MAXINE. You jumped, too, so you're stupid, too.
BETTY. Nah ah. You pinched me.
MARSHA. Why'd you pinch her?
BETTY. 'Cause she's stupid.
MAXINE. I didn't pinch you.
BETTY. Liiiee!
MARSHA. Why'd you pinch her?
MAXINE. I didn't pinch her! I swear.

BETTY. Did!

MAXINE. Didn't!

MARSHA. Okay, okay, I believe you.

BETTY. How come?

MARSHA. 'Cause I pinched you.

BETTY. Heeeey!

MAXINE. Told ya. Hey! *(To MARSHA.)* How come you didn't pinch me too?

BETTY. 'Cause I'm her best friend.

MAXINE. Nah ah!

BETTY. Uh huh!

MARSHA. Let's get some candy. *(The girls each pull up a Halloween trick or treat bag and start going through it. BETTY also pulls out her witch's hat and puts it on.)*

BETTY. We got some great stuff!

MARSHA. I love Halloween.

MAXINE. I got more'n you did.

BETTY. Nah ah!

MAXINE. Did.

BETTY. Nah ah. Lookee. *(Opens her bag and shows MAXINE.)*

MAXINE. Oooh, you're right. I didn't get a Butterfinger! *(Reaches quickly into BETTY's bag and takes the candy bar.)*

BETTY. You give me that back.

MAXINE. Now we're even.

BETTY. You give me that back!

MAXINE. What're you going to do to me if I don't?

BETTY. I'm going to pinch you!

MOTHER *(offstage voice)*. If you three don't settle down in there, the party's over and I'm going to take everybody home!

BETTY, MAXINE and MARSHA. Yeeesss maaa'aaam.

MARSHA. Let's tell some more ghost stories.
BETTY. Nah ah.
MAXINE. Uh huh.
BETTY. I get scared.
MAXINE. It's Halloween, you crouton! You're supposed to get scared.
BETTY. Yeah, but I'm not supposed to get pinched.
MAXINE. Tell Marsha, not me.
MARSHA. Okay, no more pinching. Now. Who's next?
BETTY. Not me. I don't know any scary stories.
MAXINE. You *are* a scary story.
BETTY. Nah ah!
MAXINE. Ooooh, did you hear about that girl last year, during Halloween she ate so much candy that her stomach exploded!
MARSHA and BETTY. Ohhhhh!
MARSHA. That's gross!
BETTY. That's a lie.
MAXINE. Nah ah.
BETTY. Uh huh. I never heard anything about that. That woulda been on the news and in the papers and on TV.
MAXINE. It's the truth. Happened to some congressman's daughter and they didn't put it in the papers 'cause he was running for office again.
BETTY. That's so stupid.
MARSHA. Oh, did you hear about that witch they caught?
MAXINE. Witch?
MARSHA. Uh huh.
BETTY. What witch?
MARSHA. Right here. Right here in town.
BETTY. A real witch?
MARSHA. Yeah, only she wasn't dressed like a witch. That's the scary part. She looked just like a mother.

BETTY. Nah ah.

MARSHA. She did.

MAXINE. How'd they catch her?

MARSHA. By the kind of candy she was passing out during trick or treat.

MAXINE. Trick or treat?

BETTY. What candy?

MARSHA *(all-knowing)*. Hexed candy!

MAXINE. Hexed candy?

MARSHA. Candy that was hexed. See, the way I get it, she put a spell on all the candy and then she gave it away to kids.

MAXINE. Yeah? What happened?

MARSHA. Well, the kids that ate it started...you know... changing.

MAXINE. Changing?

BETTY. Like...like for bed?

MARSHA. No. Like *into* things. The kids that ate the candy all started changing...slowly...into dolls.

MAXINE. Dolls?

MARSHA. Real ugly dolls that nobody wanted.

BETTY. Oh, I hate ugly dolls.

MARSHA. Everybody does. Anyway, how it happened is first the kids ate the candy. Then, one by one, they started changing. First, their hair started getting real curly. Then they started getting these little bumps on their arms...

MAXINE. Bumps on their arms?

MARSHA. I said they were ugly.

BETTY. But they...you said they caught the witch...didn't you?

MARSHA. Well, that's the thing, see. They caught her but had to let her go.

MAXINE. Let her go!

BETTY. How come?
MARSHA. 'Cause there's no law against ugly dolls.
BETTY. Nah ah!
MARSHA. There isn't.
MAXINE *(suddenly points)*. Betty!
BETTY. What?
MAXINE. Your hair!
BETTY. What?! What about my hair?!
MAXINE. There's a curl!
BETTY. Where?
MAXINE *(getting panicky)*. Right there, right there!
BETTY *(getting equally panicky)*. Pull it out, pull it out!
MAXINE *(reaches over to BETTY)*. Starting right there! Look!
BETTY. Pull it out, quick! Pull...Maxine! Your arms!
MAXINE *(pulls back)*. What?
BETTY. There're bumps all over them!
MAXINE. Nah ah!
BETTY. Bumps all over them. Marsha, looka here. She's... she's getting ugly!
MAXINE. Am not!
BETTY. Are so! Are so!
MAXINE. I...I wanna go home! *(She jumps up.)*
BETTY *(also jumping up)*. Me too.
BETTY and MAXINE *(calling)*. Mrs. Jackson! *(They exit quickly, leaving their trick or treat bags. MARSHA reaches over and picks up both the bags.)*
MARSHA. Works every time. *(She casually starts eating candy from one of the bags as the lights...)*

BLACKOUT

I Hate Halloween

Characters: LADY, BUTLER

(Lights come up on an old LADY sitting in a chair reading a newspaper. She is wearing a shawl and has a blanket over her legs. Her BUTLER is standing nearby.)

LADY *(lowers the paper)*. I hate Halloween.
BUTLER. Yes mum.
LADY. Look at this. Story about a girl who ate so much candy her stomach exploded.
BUTLER. Frightful.
LADY. My point exactly. What a ridiculous time of the year. All just to frighten people. Positively ridiculous.
BUTLER. If you say so, mum.
LADY. Oh. *(She squints.)* Get my glasses, will you?
BUTLER. Of course, mum. *(He exits.)*
LADY. I never heard the like. It seems to get worse every year. As if real life isn't scary enough, they have to drum up more terrors just for a celebration? It's a bunch of poppycock, if you ask me, which nobody does, of course. Trick or treaters and pumpkins carved in grotesque shapes, with gargoyle-like faces. And monsters. Of course! One night of the year and that's all you hear. Monsters! A full moon comes out and ordinary people begin changing into some sort of supernatural thing. How preposterous!

(The BUTLER enters, carrying a pair of eye glasses. However, as he reaches over and hands the glasses to the

LADY, we see his hands are now grotesque and covered with hair.)

BUTLER. Your glasses, mum.

LADY. Thank you. Did you ever see the like? Well, it's just for the merchants, you can certainly see that. Anybody with eyes in their heads who knows enough to notice what's going on around them can see that. Get my pills!

BUTLER. Yes mum. *(He exits.)*

LADY. All for the sake of the almighty cash register. Just another scam to push the merchandise. Masks and costumes and the like. Not to mention making yet another reason to have a sale on all those items they couldn't unload during regular business hours. It's a travesty, that's what it is.

(The BUTLER enters with a bottle of pills. Now his face is a grotesque hairy countenance and he walks slightly stooped over.)

BUTLER *(speech slurred)*. Your pillflls, murrm. *(He hands her the pills.)*

LADY *(taking the bottle)*. Water. How can I take my pills without water?

BUTLER. Yesfss murrm. *(He exits.)*

LADY. Oh, and let's not forget the candy makers! They must make a killing on Halloween. They start promoting it months in advance and then jack up the prices on the stuff, just before the day arrives, so you're forced to buy at their prices. It's legalized robbery! That's what it is. Legalized highway robbery!

(The BUTLER enters with a glass, half-filled with water. Now he stumbles around, ape-like, almost scampering up to the LADY. He hands her the glass.)

BUTLER. Ooojagaga!

LADY. Thank you. *(She takes the glass and starts to take her pills.)* No. I tell you what I'm going to do. I know I said I wasn't before but I'm going to do it. I'm going out. Get my things.

BUTLER. Mumph! *(He shrugs and exits.)*

LADY. It's either that or stay here and be plagued by those greedy little trick or treaters. And I, for one, am not going to stand for it any longer. Halloween, huh? They think they know what Halloween is all about, do they? *(She rises and throws off her shawl and blanket. She is wearing a black, traditional witch's outfit.)*

(The BUTLER enters carrying a witch's hat and broom. He hands them to her.)

BUTLER. Oohgalooma!

LADY *(putting on the hat)*. Try to tell *me* about trick or treat. I'll show them the way *we* used to do it back in Salem. *(She starts off and looks back at the BUTLER.)* I hate Halloween! *(She cackles and exits.)*

BLACKOUT

Out For Blood

Characters: MAN, VAMPIRE (non-speaking)

(Lights come up to find a MAN sitting in a chair. He stares off blankly into space, holding a piece of paper. Suddenly, a VAMPIRE emerges behind him, with a cape over its eyes. It sees the MAN and lowers the cape. Opening its mouth wide to expose long teeth, it moves stealthily up behind its victim. Then, sensing the right moment, it leaps on the MAN's neck and proceeds to bite it. After one bite it withdraws with a curious look on its face. The VAMPIRE tries again, and again withdraws, this time scratching its head.)

MAN. You're too late. I was just audited. *(He sadly holds up the paper. The VAMPIRE looks at it and frowns. Shaking its head, it runs a hand over the MAN's head in sympathy as the lights...)*

BLACKOUT

A Little Blackmail

Characters: MAX, LADY

(As the lights come up, a little old LADY is sitting at a table, pouring tea into a cup. She then looks at her watch and waits. There is a knock at the door. She opens it and MAX enters carrying a box.)

MAX. Excuse me.

LADY. Yes?

MAX. I...I hope I'm not intruding. I'm your neighbor.

LADY. Oh, yes, I've seen you from time to time.

MAX. My name's Max and I think we might have some business.

LADY. Oh, do sit down, please.

MAX *(sits)*. Thank you. Were...were you expecting someone?

LADY. Well, I *did* see you walking around outside.

MAX. Oh, I hope I didn't disturb you.

LADY. Not at all. I thought you might like some tea. My husband used to love tea.

MAX. Why, thank you.

LADY. I always say it doesn't hurt to go that extra yard if you can be gracious.

MAX. How very kind.

LADY. Sugar?

MAX. No. This will be fine. *(He sips the tea.)* Very good.

LADY *(sits)*. Now. How can I help you?

MAX. Well, I just thought that you and I ought to get acquainted. *(He places the box on the table.)*
LADY. Is this a gift? *(She reaches for it. MAX pulls it away.)*
MAX. In a way. But we'll come to that shortly. You know, you and this house have quite a reputation.
LADY. Oh?
MAX. Especially this time of year.
LADY. Oh, you mean all that poppycock about the place being haunted? Is that old yarn still circulating?
MAX. Something like that. *(He sips the tea again.)* Also about how your husband suddenly disappeared. If I may be so blunt.
LADY. Oh, yes, that's quite all right. I, too, have heard the stories.
MAX. So, they're just stories then?
LADY. Of course.
MAX. Well, that's a relief.
LADY. You didn't believe those stories, did you?
MAX. Of course not. But you know how people worry about property values.
LADY. Yes, I suppose. You have a dog, don't you?
MAX. Why, yes. In fact, he's the reason I'm here today.
LADY. I *thought* I saw him digging in my backyard. And it caused me a bit of worry. If he keeps digging like that he's going to hit pipes.
MAX. Well, dogs will be dogs.
LADY. Well, I hope you make sure he stops. That's the last thing I need is some neighborhood dog digging up pipes.
MAX *(suddenly menacing)*. Now, madam, let's be honest, shall we?
LADY. Honest? I don't know what you mean. I am always honest.
MAX. And I always know when opportunity knocks.

LADY. How do you mean?

MAX. Well, I know you're pretty well set up here and the thing is, I want part of it.

LADY. I beg your pardon?

MAX. I said I want part of your money.

LADY. I don't understand, young man.

MAX. Oh, just a minimal weekly paycheck...for my silence, you understand.

LADY. Your silence?

MAX. Yes. Or would you rather the authorities see this. *(He opens the box and takes out a human skull.)*

LADY. Oh my!

MAX. A little gift my dog presented to me this morning. And, I believe I can show you exactly where he dug it up...in your backyard.

LADY. Why...why, this is preposterous!

MAX. Oh, don't pretend to be so surprised. *(He sips the tea again.)*

LADY. Well, you come in here and make all sorts of demands and then you produce this...this death's head.

MAX. So, you're honest, is that what you said?

LADY. I always tell the truth. I said if your dog kept digging...

MAX *(finishing her sentence).* Yeah, I know, he'd find pipes. So, how about it? Either I get paid or I go to the cops.

LADY. Oh, you poor man, you simply don't listen.

MAX. Huh?

LADY. I told you the truth.

MAX. Lady, this is obviously your late husband and all I want...

LADY. Now, listen. I told you three things when you came in.

MAX. What three things?

LADY. Well, if you really believe this is my late husband then you obviously believe I murdered him.

MAX. Yes, but...

LADY. Three things I told you, remember?

MAX *(impatient)*. You keep saying that! What three things?!

LADY. I told you I was expecting you.

MAX. Yeah, so?

LADY. I also told you that my husband loved tea.

MAX *(starting to take a sip)*. Yeah, but...*(He gets a horrified look on his face and slams the cup back down).* You... you...

LADY *(nodding)*. That's right. You see, I saw the dog digging and knew it was only a matter of time.

MAX. But you said...*(He is gasping now.)* You said all he'd find is...

LADY. That's the third thing I told you. I said if he kept digging, he'd find pipes. You see...I am Mrs. Pipes. *(Wide-eyed, MAX stares at the LADY as the lights...)*

BLACKOUT

The Perfect Mask

Characters: MAN,
PROPRIETOR(S) [two actors recommended]

(The lights come up on the PROPRIETOR standing behind a small counter. He is resting his face on one hand. A MAN walks up.)

MAN. Good afternoon and happy Halloween.
PROPRIETOR. Happy Halloween right back to you. Welcome to Coy's Costumes. How can I help you?
MAN. Need a mask.
PROPRIETOR. Well, you've certainly come to the right place. For a party, or you just want to scare your mother-in-law out of town?
MAN. Ooh, good idea. It's for a party.
PROPRIETOR. Well, I have quite a selection under here. *(He pulls out a mask.)* What about this one? It's a holiday favorite and the Shriner's love it.
MAN. Welllll, that's okay...
PROPRIETOR. Not exactly what you're looking for?
MAN. Something a bit more realistic.
PROPRIETOR. All righty. *(He puts the mask back and takes out another one.)* What about this one? *(He hands it to the MAN.)* For awhile, I understand, they used this one in the White House.
MAN. Why'd they stop?
PROPRIETOR. Wasn't scary enough.
MAN. Look, this one's not quite right either.

PROPRIETOR. Maybe if you have some idea of what you're looking for?

MAN. Something realistic, like I said. It doesn't have to be scary, just different. See?

PROPRIETOR. Oh, something to make *you* look different.

MAN. That's right.

PROPRIETOR. But realistic.

MAN. Yes.

PROPRIETOR. Got just the thing. *(He puts his hand under his chin and ducks behind the counter. When he comes back up, his face is now horrible and hairy. He hands a flesh-colored mask to the MAN. Note: For the best results, have another man hiding behind the counter, dressed just like the PROPRIETOR but wearing the grotesque mask. Then, after the PROPRIETOR ducks down, the other man comes up.)*

MAN. That's it! Just the thing! *(He plunks down a bill and exits. The PROPRIETOR then resumes his original position, resting his chin on one hand as the lights...)*

BLACKOUT

Two Heads Are Better Than One

Characters: MOTHER, JUNIOR, DAD (non-speaking)

(As the lights come up, DAD is asleep in his favorite chair. Since his chair is turned away from the audience, we can only assume this since we hear him snoring and see his feet resting on an ottoman. MOTHER enters through a door, wiping her hands with a dish towel.)

MOTHER. Hon? Dinner's almost ready. *(She crosses to him.)* Dear? *(She looks down at him.)* Sorry. *(She smiles and pats the top of his head, which we can see over the back of the chair.)*

(JUNIOR bursts into the room.)

JUNIOR. Dad! Dad! *(MOTHER grabs him as he tries to rush by her.)*
MOTHER. Just a minute there, young man. Where do you think you're going?
JUNIOR. I need to talk to Dad.
MOTHER. He's had a hard day at the office.
JUNIOR. I won't bother him.
MOTHER. He's asleep. How're you going to ask him questions without bothering him?
JUNIOR *(guessing)*. They're real easy questions?
MOTHER. No sir. You work it out yourself.
JUNIOR. But Mom! He's the one who's always saying "Two heads are better than one."

BOO! Two Heads Are Better Than One

MOTHER. Well, he'd be the one to know, all right.

JUNIOR. I'll be real quiet, I promise.

MOTHER. No sir. You do your own homework. He's always saying that, too, you know.

JUNIOR. But this isn't homework. This is for our Halloween festival.

MOTHER. What about the Halloween festival?

JUNIOR. The kid with the best outfit wins a prize.

MOTHER. And you can't think of anything, is that it?

JUNIOR. No, not without Dad's help.

MOTHER. He helps you enough already. I swear he spoils you so.

JUNIOR. Nah *ah*!

MOTHER. Listen, you just do the best you can. And don't pout!

JUNIOR. Well, Mom, he's always saying how we don't do enough father-son stuff, isn't he?

MOTHER. Well...

JUNIOR. And wouldn't this be a great way for us to...you know...

MOTHER. Cooperate?

JUNIOR. Yeah. We'd be doing it together. Two heads are better than one.

MOTHER. Ohhh.

JUNIOR. It wouldn't hurt to ask now, would it?

MOTHER. All right. *(She walks over to DAD.)* Hon? Hon, wake up a minute, will you? *(DAD rouses himself in his chair.)*

JUNIOR. Dad? The Halloween festival is tomorrow night and I need your help with my costume. See, I want to really scare the judges.

MOTHER. Sorry, dear. He wanted to know if you'd...well, you know...kinda go along?

JUNIOR. Please, Dad. Please, please, please? *(DAD waits a minute and then raises his arms. With a slight jerk, he removes his head and hands it to JUNIOR.)* Oh, thanks, Dad. This'll be great! *(He takes the head and exits quickly out the door.)*

MOTHER. Well, I always said you'd lose your head over that boy. *(DAD points a finger at her in admonishment as the lights...)*

BLACKOUT

A Very Dirty Trick

Characters: MARK, CINDY, TOMMY,
BOBBY, MR. JACKSON

(As the lights come up, MARK and CINDY are standing, dressed in their costumes, waiting to get started trick or treating. They have their masks on top of their heads so that they can talk to each other.)

MARK. What time is it now?
CINDY. I don't know. I didn't know the last time you asked. Why do you keep asking?
MARK. Well, you're older now.
CINDY. I don't have a watch, anyway.
MARK. Maybe somebody will give you one when we get started trick or treating. *(He looks off.)* If we ever do!
CINDY. Well, why don't we just go without him?
MARK. No. Bobby said he had a great plan for this year.
CINDY. Him? A great plan?
MARK. That's what he said.
CINDY. This is the same Bobby that hung himself from a tree last year like a Shell No-Pest Strip?
MARK. I'm only telling you what he told me.
CINDY. Bobby?
MARK. You want to go ahead without us, go ahead.
CINDY. No.
MARK. All right then, stop crying.
CINDY. I'm *not* crying. I just don't want to miss trick or treat.

MARK. He'll be here. He promised.
CINDY. I wasn't crying.
MARK. No, but you were whining. Sounded like Tommy Lathrop.
CINDY. You take that back!
MARK. Yeah, okay. I just wish Bobby would...
CINDY *(looks off)*. Uh oh.
MARK. What?
CINDY. Speak of the devil.
MARK *(turns and looks)*. Bobby?
CINDY. No. Tommy Lathrop.
MARK. What?

(TOMMY enters and walks over to them.)

TOMMY *(whining)*. Oh, here you two are. I've been looking around for hooouuurs! Just hooouuuurs! Wandering around, all by myself, I was starting to get scaaaared.
CINDY. Tommy! What're you doing here?
TOMMY. Trick or treating. Won't it be fuuuunnn?
MARK. No, she means why were you looking for us? Why are you *with* us?
TOMMY. 'Caaauuuse.
MARK. 'Caaauuuse whyyyyy?
TOMMY. 'Caaauuuuse Bobby tooooold me to.
CINDY *(angrily)*. Bobby? Bobby told you to? *(She turns to MARK.)* That's his great plan?
MARK. I don't know.
CINDY. We get stuck with this whining Tommy-gun all night? That's his great plan?
MARK. I don't know, I told you. I...

(BOBBY enters and joins the group.)

BOBBY. Oh, great. Everyone's together.
CINDY. Bobby!
MARK. This is your great plan? Making Tommy go with us?
CINDY. You mean, making us go with Tommy.
BOBBY. Yeah. Don't you see the beauty part?
CINDY. What? We get in a car, put Whining Tommy on top and go as an ambulance?
BOBBY. You don't get it?
MARK. No, but *you're* going to get it in about two minutes.
TOMMY. Nobody liiiiikes me. I'm going back hoooomme. *(He starts to exit. BOBBY grabs him.)*
BOBBY. No, we like you. This is going to be your night.
TOMMY. Reeeaaally?
BOBBY. Sure. This'll be great.
MARK. How do you figure?
BOBBY. I'll show you. *(He points to R.)* There's old man Jackson's house, right?
CINDY. Right, but we weren't going to go there.
BOBBY. And why not?
CINDY. You know.
MARK. 'Cause he's such a pain, he never gives out any candy.
BOBBY. Yeah? Watch. Everybody? *(He holds out his hands like an orchestra conductor. Gives them the downbeat.)*
ALL. Trick or treat!

(After a slight beat, JACKSON enters.)

JACKSON. What is it?
ALL. Trick or treat!
JACKSON. And what if I don't go along with this juvenile blackmail?
MARK. Hah?

JACKSON. What if I don't give you any candy, you going to pull some horrible trick on me again this year?

BOBBY. No. We're going to give *you* something.

JACKSON. What? *(BOBBY shoves TOMMY at JACKSON.)*

BOBBY. Tommy Lathrop.

JACKSON *(alarmed)*. What?!

TOMMY. Helloooo, Mr. Jackson. Can I staaaaay with you toniiiight? *(JACKSON immediately pulls out a bag and starts shoveling candy into the children's sacks.)*

JACKSON. Here! Take it! Take all you want! Anything! Go ahead! *(BOBBY beams at CINDY and MARK as they nod, finally getting it.)*

MARK and CINDY. Ooooh!

BLACKOUT

A Very Sweet Treat

Characters: FIRST, SECOND, THIRD, GHOST/MARSHA

(As the lights come up four trick or treaters enter. The first THREE are dressed in various costumes but the fourth is dressed as a GHOST, totally covered by a very dusty shroud. They stop and look in their bags.)

FIRST. Okay, everybody, let's see what we have.
SECOND. Naw, let's keep going. We can count up later.
FIRST. It won't take but a minute.
THIRD. I don't think we ought to stop just yet.
FIRST. Oh, you're just scared.
THIRD. No, I'm not.
SECOND. Scared?
FIRST. On account'a there's that old cemetery back there.
SECOND *(looks back)*. Where?
FIRST *(points)*. There. We just passed it.
THIRD. I still think we ought to keep moving.
FIRST. Oh, you're just a scaredy-cat.
SECOND. It's so hard to tell out here. Let's go where there's more light and find out.
FIRST. Don't tell me you're scared too?
SECOND. I just think we ought to leave well enough alone.
FIRST. Look, we're all right as long as we three stay together.
SECOND. Okay. I guess. *(The THIRD trick or treater turns and looks at the GHOST. Then THIRD turns back.)*
THIRD. What did you just say?

FIRST. I said, we're all right as long as we three stay... *(THIRD points to the GHOST. The GHOST raises its arms and starts moaning. FIRST screams and drops his bag. SECOND turns and sees the GHOST and, along with THIRD, drops his bag. All THREE exit hastily. The GHOST then pulls off its shroud to reveal MARSHA from the second sketch.)*

MARSHA *(picks up the bags)*. Works every time. I love Halloween.

BLACKOUT

This'll Scare You To Death

Characters: DOC, JOE (doubles as GRIM REAPER),
DOLORES

(As lights come up, JOE, an old man, is sitting in a chair wearing his pajamas and robe. DOC is standing over him and checking his pulse.)

DOC. Well...*(He lets go of his arm.)*
JOE *(weakly)*. What is it, Doc?
DOC. What can I tell you, Joe, that you don't already know. *(He takes off his stethoscope and places it in his large bag.)* Your heart is barely beating and you're living on borrowed time.
JOE. Same old story, eh?
DOC. Like you'd believe me. You shouldn't be up, you know.
JOE. It's Halloween, Doc. I wanted to have one great Halloween before I shuffled off this mortal coil. *(He scowls.)* That's Shakespeare, like you'd know.
DOC. It doesn't make any sense. You're always telling me how afraid you are that one day the Grim Reaper is coming for you.
JOE. That's how I know when it's time. Been that way in my family for years.

(DOLORES enters. She is a very young, attractive woman.)

DOLORES. How is he, Doc?

DOC. Hm? Oh. He's...as well as can be expected.

DOLORES. He's going to get well, I just know he is. *(She leans over to JOE.)* No husband of mine is going to just give up, now is he?

JOE. I'll know when it's time. One great Halloween, that's all I want. *(He tries to get up.)* Doc, help me, will you?

DOC *(helps JOE to his feet)*. We'll get you back to bed where you belong.

JOE. I was hoping that we'd get a few trick or treaters tonight.

DOC. That's about all you'd need. One great costume and your heart wouldn't take it.

DOLORES. Oh, did he tell you that old story about his family and the Grim Reaper?

JOE. It ain't no story, Dolores.

DOLORES *(patronizingly)*. Of course not, dear. You get back into bed, why don't you?

JOE. I'm going, I'm going.

DOC. All right. Take it easy. *(DOC helps JOE exit through a door. DOLORES waits for them to leave and then pulls out a document.)*

DOLORES *(looking at the document)*. All legal and taken care of. "Sound of mind and body." Hah! One great Halloween, he says. Well, he's going to get one great Halloween all right. One that'll scare him to death.

(DOC re-enters.)

DOLORES. Is he?

DOC. He's resting in bed now but he's still awake.

DOLORES. Good. We want him awake.

DOC. Right. *(They embrace in a loving kiss.)*

DOLORES *(breaking the kiss)*. Now. You have everything?

DOC. You know I do. *(He opens his bag and takes out a large black robe and skeletal mask.)* I figure about the time I get this on, he ought to be ready for me. *(He proceeds to put the costume on.)*

DOLORES. This is the perfect scheme. The will gives everything to me.

DOC. And me.

DOLORES. Right. Then you go in there and wham! He's gone to his just rewards and leaves us *our* just rewards.

DOC. And suppose I *don't* scare him to death?

DOLORES. We've been over that. We just convince him later that he was hallucinating. New medication, right?

DOC. I guess. What about the rest of his family?

DOLORES. Doesn't have any, as far as I know. We got married so quickly, remember?

DOC. It's like you had this planned all along.

DOLORES. I thought of everything, all right. Now. Get in there and let's get this over with.

DOC *(now in full costume)*. Right. *(He holds out his arms and exits through the bedroom door.)*

DOLORES. The next sound you hear...? *(She listens attentively. She hears sounds of DOC moaning.)*

JOE *(offstage)*. What...who're you? Who...?! Ah! No! AAAHHHHHH!

(There is a long silence. Finally, DOC emerges from the room. He is breathing heavily.)

DOLORES. Well?

DOC. Let me catch my breath. *(He takes off the mask and sits in the chair.)*

DOLORES. Oh, what happened? Is he...?

DOC *(nods)*. He's dead. No pulse.

DOLORES. Good. I *knew* it would work. Even if it didn't, we could've always told him we were just going along with his wish to have one more great Halloween. *(She looks back at DOC.)* What? What's wrong?

DOC. Nothing...only...

DOLORES. Only what?

DOC. It's just...his face. That horrible expression.

DOLORES. What did you expect?

DOC *(rises)*. I...I didn't know quite *what* to expect. I know I'll never forget his face, though.

DOLORES. Don't worry, I'll buy you a lot of *other* faces.

DOC. No, I mean it! You should see him!

DOLORES. There'll be time for that at the funeral. *(Disgusted.)* Will you get hold of yourself? So, he looked scared, what did you expect?

DOC. That's just it. He didn't have a frightened look. It wasn't a fearful expression.

DOLORES. Well, what, then?

DOC. It was more one of...of revenge.

DOLORES. Revenge? He's dead!

DOC. But his expression, the *way* he died...

DOLORES. Listen, forget him. *(She hugs him.)* We own everything now. Just you and me. Don't tell me about revenge.

DOC. But you should see him. It's as if he's...*(There is a knock at the front door. DOC jumps.)*

DOLORES. Will you get hold of yourself?

DOC. Who could that be?

DOLORES. Trick or treaters. It's Halloween, remember? Get it, will you?

DOC. Oh. Right.

(DOC moves to the door and opens it. The GRIM REAPER enters.)

DOC. What the...*(He backs away.)* You stay away from me. *(The REAPER moves closer to him.)* No! Stay away from me I said!

DOLORES. Will you control yourself! Look! *(She rushes up to the REAPER and pulls off its hood.)* You. Take off that mask. *(The REAPER removes the mask to reveal JOE.)*

DOC *(shaking with fear)*. What? You can't! You *can't* be back! You're...you're...*(He backs into the room and clutches his heart. He falls to the floor, dead. DOLORES moves away from JOE.)*

DOLORES. It *can't* be! You...you stay away from me! It *can't* be you! It *can't*! No! NOOOOO! *(She runs screaming out of the room through the open front door. JOE leans down and feels for a pulse on DOC's arm. He then drops the arm and rises again.)*

JOE. Hm. I guess Joe never told them he had a twin brother.

BLACKOUT

Grave Situation

Characters: PHIL, MAC

(As lights come up, MAC is sitting on a bench. Next to him is a tombstone covered with a large sack. MAC is checking his long-handled shovel. PHIL enters with a shovel over his shoulder.)

PHIL. I thought I'd find you here.

MAC. Shovel head worked loose. I thought if I could wedge something down between the wood and the sleeve it'd hold up till we got through here today.

PHIL. Good excuse as any. *(He sits.)*

MAC. No excuse. Look. *(He holds up the shovel.)* Still got a wobble to it.

PHIL. You really get me, old man.

MAC. How's 'at?

PHIL. Here you go out and dig graves all day, day in and day out and the only thing that bothers you is a wobbly shovel.

MAC. Well, it ain't only digging the graves that keeps me busy. I got that other sideline going for me. *(He indicates the covered tombstone.)*

PHIL. Making tombstones. Yeah, I know. Still, you're a pretty hard crock, ain't ya?

MAC. I do what has to be done. *(He looks back.)* Never had no complaints neither.

PHIL. Not from that crowd, that's for sure.

MAC. Nobody does much questioning. They just glad old Mac here does the job.

PHIL. Well, maybe you ain't doing the job to suit them anymore.

MAC. How's 'at?

PHIL. I just said maybe you're getting too old for the work. That's why they hired me, you know.

MAC. I could get the job done, if left to it.

PHIL. Well, maybe not. *(He rises.)* That's why they hired me to help you.

MAC. Don't need no help.

PHIL. Well, you got it, old man. Didn't I as much as dig that one over there, all by myself?

MAC. Shovel head was loose.

PHIL. That ain't the only head that's loose, if you ask me.

MAC. Ask who?

PHIL. Me. Phillip Jones. *(He leans in.)* The man what's about to take over your job, old man!

MAC. What? *(He looks up.)*

PHIL. That's right. They told me today. Town council. Said I was to take over the job.

MAC. S'that a fact.

PHIL. That's a fact. I didn't want to let on nothing on account'a I wanted to make sure it was certain. See, I been planning this all along. Jobs is hard to come by. So I staked out this one. A little manual labor, I call my own hours. Well, you know all about it. So I says to myself, all I got to do is make you look bad. That was probably the easiest part of the job. Then I make my move and I'm set for life.

MAC. So you had come up with your little plan?

PHIL. That's right. And it worked out pretty good, if you ask me. *(Stares at MAC.)* You don't seem too upset about it.

MAC. Well, maybe it ain't the first time the council said that.

PHIL. It's the first time they're going to go through with it.

MAC. With you?

PHIL. That's right. Me.

MAC. Phillip Ray Tomkins?

PHIL. That's right...wait. My name's Jones. I done told you that...

MAC. I know what you told me. I know what you told the council. Drifter comes into town and spots a job he can ease into without nobody asking no questions.

PHIL. It's Jones, I tell you!

MAC. Maybe the council don't do no questioning but old Mac does.

PHIL. How'd you find out?

MAC. I got my ways. I do what has to be done. Remember, I told you?

PHIL *(moves behind MAC)*. But you're the only one that knows, right?

MAC. I keeps to myself. I got my own records right up here in my head.

PHIL. And nobody to confide in, neither, right?

MAC. All by myself in this world. Just like you. *(Suddenly PHIL makes a lunge at MAC who rises quickly, eluding PHIL's grasp.)*

PHIL. You gonna turn me in? I didn't have no part in that fire last year, you know.

MAC. Didn't say I was gonna turn you in, now did I?

PHIL. Yeah, but how can I be sure?

MAC. You can't.

PHIL. One way I can. *(He takes out a knife and moves to MAC.)* This way.

MAC. You get rid of me. Think it's that easy?

PHIL. Why not? It's a good plan. I take over after I've gotten rid of you. Tell the council that you got mad at being fired and up and left town!

MAC. Say, that is a pretty good plan. *(He backs over to the tombstone.)* Only one little change.

PHIL *(moves to him)*. What's that?

MAC. This. *(He pulls out a revolver and shoots PHIL. PHIL drops the knife and falls, clutching to the tombstone.)* See? I told you this weren't the first time the council thought of this. Only this time I was ready for them.

PHIL. Ready for them? How...how do you mean?

MAC. Maybe I ain't so old as you'd like to think. Maybe I had a little plan, too. See, it's you that will suddenly disappear. I'll just say that you, being a drifter, just up and left. Who's to wonder why?

PHIL. But what about...you can't get away with it. They'll try to find me.

MAC. You took care of that. They'll be looking for Phillip Jones. There must be thousands of Joneses.

PHIL. No. *(He is fading.)* You can't...

MAC. Oh, don't worry. I got you a nice little spot picked out. You just dug it yourself.

PHIL. What?!!

MAC. I told you. *(He pulls off the tombstone cover to reveal the lettering, which reads:* PHILLIP RAY TOMKINS, REST IN PEACE.*)* I do what needs to be done.

PHIL. No! NOOOO! *(Lights fade to...)*

BLACKOUT

Better Late Than Never

Characters: LYDIA, CHARLEY, PHOEBE

(As lights come up, there is no one in the scene. Then the door opens and CHARLEY enters. He crosses to the chair and falls into it. LYDIA enters through the other door.)

LYDIA. You're home.//
CHARLEY. No, I'm a ghost.//
LYDIA. Terrible joke, dear. *(She kisses him on the forehead.)*//
CHARLEY *(rises)*. Just keeping with the season. Where's my newspaper?//
LYDIA. Under your arm.//
CHARLEY *(finds it)*. Oh yeah. *(He hands the paper to LYDIA while he takes off his tie and jacket.)* What a day. One thing after another.//
LYDIA. None of which you want to talk about, I'm sure.//
CHARLEY. I'm sure. You never like it when I do, anyway.//
LYDIA. No, it's when you bring your work home. *That's* when I object.//
CHARLEY. Oh ho, and *my* joke was bad?//
LYDIA. What? What did I say?//
CHARLEY. You just said you hate it when I bring my work home.//
LYDIA. So?//
CHARLEY. You're telling a mortician you hate it when he brings...//
LYDIA. Oh no! Not that! I meant all your paperwork and... and that reminds me. Somebody called for you.

CHARLEY. Work?

LYDIA. She sounded like it. Said she just missed you down at the mortuary.

CHARLEY. Did you get a number?

LYDIA. She hung up before I could.

CHARLEY. Well, I'll deal with it tomorrow.

LYDIA. Whatever you think. Dinner'll be ready in about fifteen minutes. *(She exits, carrying CHARLEY's tie and jacket. CHARLEY relaxes in his chair with his newspaper. After a brief pause, there is a knock at the front door.)*

CHARLEY. Who's there? *(Another knock.)* Who's there? *(He rises and crosses to the door.)* Who is it? *(Another knock.)* Oh!

(CHARLEY opens the door and PHOEBE enters.)

PHOEBE. Mr. Blatt?

CHARLEY. Yes?

PHOEBE. Blatt of the Cracken, Blatt and Potter Mortuary?

CHARLEY. That's right. Can I help you?

PHOEBE. Well, I'm afraid I'm in need of your services.

CHARLEY. Oh? Did you call earlier?

PHOEBE. Yes. May I sit down?

CHARLEY. Oh, of course.

PHOEBE. I like the name of your establishment. Cracken, Blatt and Potter. Sounds like a noise you'd get by pouring milk over your cereal.

CHARLEY. Ma'am, I really don't have all my materials here at home, so I don't see...

PHOEBE. Oh, you sound just like my husband. My late husband. He was always accusing me of waiting till the last moment to get things done.

CHARLEY. Well, in my business, that's not unheard of, Mrs...?

PHOEBE. Oh, I haven't introduced myself, have I? I'm Phoebe deWolf.

CHARLEY. I see. *(He takes a pad out of his shirt pocket and begins writing.)* DeWolf?

PHOEBE. Small "de," big "Wolf." 1713 Ravenhurst.

CHARLEY. Well, I guess I can go over the basics now and we can finalize the details in the morning.

PHOEBE. I would like your least expensive package.

CHARLEY. For this you came over to my house.

PHOEBE. Now, as to the box.

CHARLEY. Mrs. deWolf, we like to think of them as sleep chambers.

PHOEBE. Sleep chambers cost too much. Box sounds a lot cheaper. Do they still make those pine things?

CHARLEY. Not since Wyatt Earp.

PHOEBE. Well, anything with the barest of essentials.

CHARLEY. Right. *(He writes this down.)* You would like a lid, right?

PHOEBE. Is it necessary?

CHARLEY. Well, when they begin to throw the dirt on the box...I mean the sleep chamber...

PHOEBE. I see your point. Fine. Put a lid on it.

CHARLEY. Now, as to a monument.

PHOEBE. Nope.

CHARLEY. Tombstone?

PHOEBE. Afraid not.

CHARLEY. You want us to nail two sticks together? You bring the sticks, we'll provide the nail.

PHOEBE. Must there be a grave marker?

CHARLEY. It's the law, lady.

PHOEBE. Very well.

CHARLEY. We have a beautiful grey marble.
PHOEBE. Too much.
CHARLEY. Pink marble?
PHOEBE. What's the cheapest?
CHARLEY *(writes it)*. Brick.
PHOEBE. Perfect.
CHARLEY. I want you to go shopping with my wife sometime. Now. Choir? *(PHOEBE shakes her head.)* Mourners?
PHOEBE. Just whoever's in the neighborhood at the time.
CHARLEY. Look, lady, we can't charge *them!*
PHOEBE. No choir, no mourners.
CHARLEY. How about the service?
PHOEBE. Well, what is it? Twenty-five words or less, I mean.
CHARLEY. This ain't a telegram.
PHOEBE. Something short.
CHARLEY. How about "Good luck in your new location."
PHOEBE. Now. What kinda gas mileage does your hearse get?
CHARLEY. You've thought of everything, haven't you?
PHOEBE. Well, I tried. *(She looks at her watch.)* Oh, I have to leave. They're very exact about these things. I'll see you at the city morgue in the morning. *(She rushes to the door.)*
CHARLEY. Yes ma'am, but I still need...
PHOEBE. You can take care of the rest. I'm sure you'll know what to do. *(She exits.)*
CHARLEY. Mrs. deWolf!

(LYDIA enters from the kitchen.)

CHARLEY. Mrs. deWolf?
LYDIA *(picks up the paper)*. Who was that?
CHARLEY. Ebenezer Scrooge in a dress.

LYDIA *(thumbing through the paper)*. I bet that was the lady who called here earlier.

CHARLEY. That was her. One Phoebe deWolf.

LYDIA *(stops at a page and stares at it)*. One Phoebe deWolf of 1713 Ravenhurst?

CHARLEY. That's her. Trying to get everything done at the last minute.

LYDIA. You can say that again.

CHARLEY. What?

LYDIA *(handing the paper to CHARLEY)*. She died early this morning.

CHARLEY *(grabs the paper)*. What? *(He stares at the paper and slowly sits in his chair.)* This can't be. Why do I get all the nuts! *(He raises the paper and reads it.)*

LYDIA. There you go again. You're just imagining it all. Thinking everybody's out to get you.

CHARLEY. I'm not imagining it.

LYDIA. Yes, you are. By the way, hon…knock knock? *(CHARLEY slowly lowers the newspaper and looks at LYDIA as the lights dim to…)*

BLACKOUT
END OF ACT ONE

ACT TWO
Her Last Possession

Based on a story by
Rose Ann Cook

Characters: LINDA, JASON, HILDA, BARBARA,
            WITCH (may be played by Hilda or Barbara)

(The living room of JASON and LINDA MUIR. The room has two practical doors. One, L, is the front door and leads to the outside. The second door leads to the kitchen. A small staircase, UC, leads to the second story and bedrooms. The furniture, while very ordinary, is comfortable and warm. A couch and coffee table are located at an angle just off C. Near it is a chair and small side table, which holds a telephone. There is a fireplace U of the kitchen door. The rest of the room is rounded out with various knickknacks, such as plants, lamps and other small pieces of furniture. Also around the room are Halloween decorations, and there is a cassette player on the mantle.

Before the lights come up, eerie music is heard. Then, a lighted jack-o'lantern seems to float, face out, down the stairs. It stops at the bottom and we hear a very evil and long laugh. Then...)

LINDA *(offstage)*. Jay? *(The grinning pumpkin turns toward the voice.)*
JASON. What?

LINDA. Will you turn on the lights down there?
JASON. Got my hands full. Hit the stair switch, will you?

(After a slight pause, the lights come up and we see it was JASON who was holding the pumpkin as he came down the stairs. He gleefully places the gourd on the coffee table, still facing out.)

LINDA. How's it look?
JASON. Great. Come see.

(LINDA enters down the stairs.)

LINDA. I swear, you get worse every year.
JASON. Practice, dear, practice. How about on the mantle? *(He starts to pick the jack-o'lantern up.)*
LINDA *(stops him)*. It's fine right where it is. What, you want to mount it over the fireplace like some moose head?
JASON. Ooh, where can we get a moose head?
LINDA. Never mind. Sorry I said anything. *(She crosses to the cassette player on the mantle and turns off the music.)*
JASON. Oh, why'd you turn off the music?
LINDA. Music? You call that music?
JASON. Sure. *(He turns it back on.)* Listen, dear. They're playing our song. *(He takes her arms and they dance.)*
LINDA. I think maybe in your past life you were a vampire.
JASON *(doing Bela Lugosi)*. Vat do you mean, my passst liiiffe. Rowrrr! *(He bites her neck.)*
LINDA *(pulls away)*. Will you stop! *(She again shuts off the music.)*
JASON. Something wrong?
LINDA. No. It's just that...you always get carried away with Halloween. You *can* be a bit weird, you know.

JASON *(hugs her)*. Only when the moon is just right. We'll get everything set up and we're all going to sit around the fire, tell ghost stories, hand treats out at the door, just like always.

LINDA. Ooh, can't you feel it? It's cold in here. Been like that all afternoon.

JASON. Shame we don't live in Salem. We could just throw another witch on the fire.

LINDA. Jay!

JASON. All right. No more spooky. *(He looks at her.)* You sure there's nothing else bothering you?

LINDA. No. *(She moves away.)* Well...

JASON. I knew it. You invited your mother over and you're afraid she'll scare the kids off.

LINDA *(glares at him)*. She likes you.

JASON. And I like her and you know it. Come on. What is it?

LINDA. Well, you know that we never did find a frame for Barbara's graduation portrait. I mean, a nice one.

JASON. What about the one I made? *(He begins arranging the decorations.)*

LINDA. The papier-mâché one?

JASON. She liked it.

LINDA. Yeah, and what happens if it ever gets wet?

JASON. She's not going to shower with the thing. *(He turns.)* You got it wet, didn't you? Threw it in the washer, something like that?

LINDA. No! It's still intact. But I bought another frame. It... well, it was a bit more than I wanted to spend. But it's perfect. *(She moves to the kitchen door.)* You'll see. I hid it in the kitchen until I could tell you about it...*(She exits into the kitchen.)*

JASON. I can't believe she doesn't like papier-mâché. And she thinks *I'm* weird. *(He yells to LINDA.)* Do I need to close my eyes?

LINDA *(offstage)*. I'm coming!

(LINDA enters with a box. She opens the box and takes out a framed picture of Barbara. The frame is obviously very old and made of some sort of dark, carved wood.)

LINDA. Here. Isn't it beautiful?

JASON. Ooh. It *is* nice. What kind of wood is that?

LINDA. The girl didn't know. She said it was part of some estate sale. I think it was her first day. She didn't have any idea how much it was so I made an offer and she took it.

JASON. Great. I hate to admit it...wait a minute. She didn't know how much to charge for the frame and *you* made an offer?

LINDA. Yeah.

JASON. And we overpaid for it?

LINDA *(changing the subject)*. Look at the wood. Look at the carving along here.

JASON. Okay, okay, no more questions. But if Barbara wants the other frame, the one I made by the sweat of my brow...

LINDA *(interrupting him)*. Is *that* what held it together?

JASON. You know what I mean.

LINDA. Fine. But I think this frame might be worth something. Look at it. It's almost compelling...sort of.

JASON. I suppose. *(He props the framed picture on the mantle.)* It does seem to draw your gaze. I mean, it's almost hypnotic the way it...*(He gazes hard at it as does LINDA. Then, as if breaking a trance, they look at each other and laugh.)* Well, if you like it, we'll keep it no matter what.

LINDA. Good. *(She moves toward the kitchen.)*

JASON. By the way, where's the frame I made?
LINDA. Have the garbage men been here yet? *(She exits into the kitchen.)*
JASON. I think they...HEEEEY! *(Looks around the room.)* Wait. Where's my skull? Oh yeah! *(He exits up the stairs and the eerie music suddenly comes on.)*

(After a beat or two, LINDA enters from the kitchen.)

LINDA. Jay, I turned that junk off for a reason, I...*(She sees she is alone. Shrugging, she again turns off the cassette player.)*

(JASON comes down the stairs carrying a plastic human skull. He places it on the mantle.)

JASON. Why'd you turn the music on and off?
LINDA. I turned it off because it was getting on my nerves. *You* turned it on.
JASON. No, I didn't.
LINDA. Oh, right.
JASON. Linda, I ran upstairs to get this. *(He points at the skull.)* The music came on after I left. How...? *(He looks at her and grins.)* Oh, I get it.
LINDA. You get what?
JASON. And you're always saying how you hate spooky stuff. *(He puts his arm around her.)* I'm so proud.
LINDA *(pulls away)*. I didn't turn it on.
JASON. Well, it didn't turn itself on. *(He looks around at the player. LINDA is right behind him. They move closer to the it. JASON reaches slowly over to turn the player on... and the phone rings. They both jump.)* Ah!
LINDA. It's the phone.

JASON *(crossing to phone)*. Right. *(He picks up the receiver.)* Hello, Halloween headquarters. Barbara? What? You are?

LINDA *(moves to JASON)*. Is it Barbara?

JASON *(nods)*. Calling from her car phone. She's coming home for the weekend. *(Back to the phone.)* Hah? Great! Right, we'll be right here. *(He hangs up.)*

LINDA. This is rather sudden.

JASON. Nah, you know how much she loves this time of year. Said she's about ten minutes away.

LINDA. Rather hasty decision, wasn't it?

JASON. Hasty decision? Hon, she just got the idea and jumped in her car. About three hours ago, she said.

LINDA *(moves to the mantle)*. About the time I...about the time I bought that frame.

JASON. Ooh, spooky enough for me! *(He takes the frame off the mantle.)* Here. We ought to hide it. *(He tries to give it to LINDA.)* Then when she gets here...What?

LINDA. *You* hide it.

JASON. Oh, you sure you're not superstitious? *(He crosses to the stairs.)*

LINDA. No, knock wood.

JASON. Right. *(He exits up the stairs. LINDA moves to the mantle. She stares at the cassette player. Slowly, she reaches out and just before her finger touches the button, the doorbell rings. She jumps.)*

LINDA. Ah! *(She calms herself. The doorbell rings again.)* I'll get it! *(She crosses to the door.)* It can't be Barbara already. I wonder who...

(LINDA opens the door and HILDA enters.)

HILDA *(holding a receipt)*. Excuse me, I hope I am not intruding. I am looking for Mrs. Linda Muir.

LINDA *(still nervous)*. I'm her. I'm me. That's I. *(She calms herself.)* I'm...Linda Muir.

HILDA. Mrs. Muir, this morning you came into my store and purchased a frame?

LINDA. Oh, *you* run that little shop? I've often passed that place and wondered about it. So, this morning I went in and...oh, won't you sit down?

HILDA *(moves slowly into the room)*. I won't be long.

LINDA. Your shop is de*light*ful. I must get Jay to come in there. I've seen antique stores before but...

HILDA *(urgently)*. The frame, Mrs. Muir. I must have it back. It wasn't for sale.

LINDA. What?

HILDA. Gloria sold it accidentally. I had told her that it wasn't for sale but, well, you know how young people are these days. They never listen. That frame was...that is to say, I had been showing it to a close friend before you came in. As a display piece, you might say. Then when I got back from lunch, Gloria told me you came in and purchased it. You see how it is.

LINDA. But didn't it come from an estate sale?

HILDA. Yes, that's true. But, as I said, it's not for sale.

(JASON comes down the stairs.)

JASON. Who is it, dear?

LINDA. Hon, this is...oh, I'm sorry, you didn't...

HILDA. Krolex. Hilda Krolex. I own the store where your wife bought a frame this morning.

JASON. Oh, it's great! One in a million.

LINDA *(crosses to JASON)*. Jay, there's a small problem. Miss...Krolex says it wasn't for sale.

JASON. Oh, come on. *Everything's* for sale.

HILDA. Normally, sir, I would agree with you. After all, you and I are business people, are we not?

JASON. Sort of. I'm a lawyer.

HILDA. Lawyer? Oh, don't tell me that.

LINDA. She wants the frame back.

HILDA. Mr. Muir, I shall be glad to refund your money.

JASON. Wait a minute. Wait just one little minute here. *(He moves away from HILDA.)* This is going a bit fast for me. Is it more money you're after?

HILDA. No, sir, I assure you.

JASON. Because you're not going to get it. We bought and paid for the frame and we have a bill of sale to prove it.

LINDA. Jay!

HILDA. I'm very well aware of that, sir, if you'll just listen.

JASON. I get it. Your girl undersold it, is that it?

HILDA. No, sir. Please, you must let me buy it back.

JASON. That's it. You got another buyer. Someone willing to pay a bundle?

HILDA. I told you, sir, the frame is not for sale. At *any* price.

JASON. You're right about that. Because now *we* own it.

LINDA. Jay, there's no need to be rude.

JASON. Part of the job, dear.

HILDA. He's a lawyer, all right.

JASON. Now, I'm sorry if you didn't get your price, miss, but the fact is the deal has been made.

HILDA. You don't know what you're doing.

JASON. Well, that's not the *first* time I've heard that.

HILDA. I'm thinking of you and your family, sir. You *must* believe me.

LINDA. Jay, I think she's serious.

JASON. Well, we're keeping the frame and we thank you for your support. You can take us to court if you like but there are laws providing for just this sort of thing.

HILDA. There are also laws, I daresay, you know nothing about.

JASON. Meaning?

HILDA. Meaning if you keep it, I can assure you, you will regret it.

JASON. Is that a threat?

LINDA. Jay, why don't we just give...

JASON. No. I will not be threatened in my own home. Miss Krolex, I must ask you to leave.

HILDA. I'll give you a profit. I don't make much...

JASON. It's not for sale.

HILDA. You cannot keep that frame!

JASON. Miss Krolex, if you don't...!

HILDA. It's cursed! *(An unsettling silence falls over the room.)*

LINDA *(breaking the tension)*. You should've seen the one he made.

JASON. What did you say?

HILDA. I said...the frame is cursed. If you *are* to keep the frame, you should know the consequences. It has...properties about it. Look. I got the frame through a bidding company. They had acquired an estate belonging to Elzbeth Lorvack. Does the name mean anything to you?

JASON. Can't say it does.

HILDA *(crosses to the fireplace)*. They had pieces on the news. Sort of fillers, I think they call them. Elzbeth Lorvack was known to everyone in upstate as a practicing witch.

JASON. A practicing witch? *(He looks at LINDA.)* Oh, I get it now. You two set this thing up, right? Getting a little of my own back on Halloween?

LINDA. Hon, I promise you I don't know anything about this.

HILDA. Lorvack died but even *that* is still unconfirmed. They never found a body. You see...*(She turns back to them.)* Her house burned down. Only a few pieces escaped, that frame being one of them. And what remained was destroyed by some of the neighbors. No one knew about the frame because it was taken away before it, too, was burned along with the rest.

JASON *(crosses to her)*. And you just happened to get it?

HILDA. How I got it is not important. *(JASON turns away.)* All right. Answer me this. Since you brought it home, haven't certain things been happening? Certain unexplained things?

JASON. No, of course not.

(The front door opens and BARBARA enters, carrying a suitcase.)

BARBARA. Trick or treat! *(LINDA and JASON cross to her.)*

LINDA. Hon!

BARBARA. It's great to be back.

JASON. It's about time you got here. *(He takes her suitcase.)*

BARBARA. I just had to come. Our time of year, right, Dad?

JASON. Her father's daughter.

LINDA. Oh, Barbara, this is Miss Krolex.

BARBARA. Hello.

JASON. Yeah, she was just telling us all about a frame Mom bought.

BARBARA. A frame? *(With distaste.)* Brother, it's stuffy in here. You two ought to air the place out. It's like the inside of a coffin.

HILDA. Inside of a what?

BARBARA *(stops and thinks)*. Odd. I meant to say attic. I said coffin, didn't I? What's this about a frame?

BOO! Her Last Possession   Page 59

JASON. I'll get it. *(He exits up the stairs.)*
LINDA. It's to replace the one your father made.
BARBARA. Thank God. How are you, Mom? *(They hug.)*
HILDA. Have...have you already put a picture in the frame?
LINDA. Yes. Barbara's. Why?
HILDA. You must remove it! You can keep the frame but take the picture out of it!
LINDA. What?
BARBARA. What's all this about? *(She staggers a bit.)* Whoa, what in the world...?
LINDA. Barbara? *(She catches her and helps her to the sofa.)* What is it? Are you all right?
BARBARA. Oh, I'm fine. I just got a little woozy. Probably from the traffic fumes.
HILDA. It's working already! Mrs. Muir, you must believe me!
BARBARA. What is she talking about?
LINDA *(now determined)*. She's...she's come to get her frame back. *(She moves to the stairs.)* Jay! Jay, get down here with that...

(JASON comes down the stairs holding the frame.)

JASON. Okay. What's the gag?
LINDA. What?
JASON. Who's been fooling around with this thing?
HILDA. It's happening!
LINDA. Nobody's touched it. You took it upstairs.
JASON. Yeah, well, I didn't do this. *(He turns the picture around. Now, instead of Barbara's picture, there is the portrait of an old, wrinkled, evil-looking woman. Just as JASON turns the frame around, the eerie music begins to*

play. LINDA rushes over and shuts the player off. She turns and glares at JASON.)

LINDA. I think we have to return that frame to Mrs. Krolex.

JASON. What? Barbara, we had your picture in here and... What's wrong, hon?

BARBARA. I...I feel weak, Daddy. *(She tries to get up but can't.)* I don't seem to have any energy all of a sudden.

HILDA. It's not energy you're losing, it's your will.

JASON. Look, I've had about enough of you! You've caused enough trouble here for one day!

LINDA. Jason! Help Barbara up to her room.

JASON. Right. *(To HILDA.)* You be gone when I get back. *(He moves to BARBARA and, after placing the picture on the coffee table, helps her to her feet.)* Come on, shug. A little nap and then we'll start a fire and begin telling ghost stories.

BARBARA. That's why I came home. I just wish I felt better.

JASON. You'll be fine. A little nap and you'll be fine. *(They exit up the stairs. LINDA waits until they've gone, then snatches up the frame and shoves it at HILDA.)*

LINDA. Take it! Take it away from here!

HILDA *(backs away)*. It's...it's too late. The spell is already working.

LINDA. What do you mean? You get this thing out of here! Now! This minute!

HILDA. I can't! Don't you see? Elzbeth's already changed the picture.

LINDA. But if you take the frame now...

HILDA. She has made contact with her medium! That picture gave her access. Her spirit has found her gateway back into this world. It wouldn't make any difference if I *did* take the frame back. She will take over Barbara's will.

LINDA. How can you be sure?

HILDA. I'm sure. Just take it from me, I'm sure. *(She moves away from LINDA.)* If I could get her back into the frame...

LINDA. If we take the picture out of the frame...! *(She tries to pull the picture out but HILDA stops her immediately.)*

HILDA. No! That's exactly what you can*not* do. That's what the witch wants you to do! We have to get her to leave the picture and return to the frame. And maybe I know how.

LINDA. How?

HILDA. Family secret.

LINDA. Fam...you mean?

HILDA. Elzbeth Lorvack...was my grandmother. You see that now, don't you? You see why I cannot ever sell or give the frame away. It's like some deadly legacy. My family is responsible. I *must* prevail.

LINDA. Why not just burn the frame?

HILDA. To destroy it might only release her spirit. I...I can't take the chance.

LINDA. Look. What can we do now? We're running out of time.

HILDA. Yes, yes, you're absolutely right.

LINDA. What do we need?

HILDA. You can only kill the past *with* the past.

LINDA. What do you mean?

(JASON comes down the stairs.)

JASON. Linda, I'm going to call Doctor Gerterson. Barbara seems to be in some sort of half sleep. I've never seen anything like it.

HILDA. It won't do you any good.

JASON *(phone in his hand)*. You still here?

LINDA. Jason, listen to her.

JASON. What *is* it with you two? If I find out that the three of you set this up...

HILDA. Look, if you don't believe in any of this, and I can't say I blame you, then humor me.

JASON. But my daughter is obviously very sick. If I don't call the doctor...

HILDA. Call him. *(To LINDA.)* It might be a good idea in the long run.

LINDA *(takes the phone).* I'll do it. *(She dials.)*

HILDA. But please, Mr. Muir. Allow me to tend to her until he gets here. Is that asking too much?

JASON. Tend to her?

HILDA. Take care of her until the doctor gets here.

JASON. You're really serious, aren't you? *(He takes a deep breath.)* What're you going to do?

HILDA. A few waves of the arms, a couple of ancient incantations, what can it hurt?

JASON. Incantations?

HILDA. Some words, some phrases from the past. What've you got to lose?

JASON. This is getting silly.

HILDA. There's nothing silly about it. Now. I need a large mixing bowl and a wooden spoon. Also, do you have any garlic, fresh dirt, and anything freshly killed?

JASON. I was wrong. *Now* it's getting silly.

HILDA. I have the book in my van. *(LINDA gets off the phone.)*

LINDA. He's being paged. Now, what do we need?

JASON. Oh, not much. Eye of newt, wing of bat and, oh yeah, have you run over anything with the car lately?

HILDA. I'll be right back. Don't touch the frame, whatever you do. *(She exits out the front door.)*

LINDA. What did she say? What do we need?

BOO! Her Last Possession   Page 63

JASON. I can't believe I'm doing this.
LINDA. Jay!
JASON. Uhmmm, a mixing bowl, a large one, and a wooden spoon.
LINDA. I'll get it. *(She exits into the kitchen. After she leaves, JASON slowly moves to the frame and picks it up. He scratches his chin, thinking. Getting an idea, he turns the frame over, trying to get the picture out.)*

(LINDA enters, carrying a bowl and spoon.)

LINDA *(sees him)*. No! *(JASON drops the frame at her scream.)*
JASON. What?!
LINDA. You heard her! *(She places the bowl on the coffee table and picks up the frame.)*
JASON. You almost scared me to death.
LINDA. What else?
JASON. Hah?
LINDA. What else do we need?
JASON. Oh. something about garlic, dirt...
LINDA. The garlic is in the kitchen. Get it, hon. It's in the pantry next to the sugar.
JASON. I don't believe we're playing along with this...*(He exits through the kitchen door.)*
LINDA *(thinking)*. Dirt...dirt. *(She remembers.)* Potting soil! I have a potted plant...*(She exits out the front door.)*

(After a slight pause, BARBARA enters down the stairs. She is very relaxed, with a sinister smile on her lips.)

BARBARA. I must find out who owns this place. Till then, I shall keep my own counsel. *(She sees the frame and picks it up.)* Ah, my spiritual vessel. And a jack-o'lantern. How apropos.

(JASON enters, carrying a small bottle of garlic.)

JASON. Barbara! *("BARBARA" looks behind her and then realizes he is speaking to her.)*
BARBARA. Oh! Yes?
JASON. You're...you're all right. *(He hugs her. She complies, clumsily.)*
BARBARA. Just needed a good rest. That's all.
JASON *(breaking the hug)*. I was really worried about you.
BARBARA. How kind. What's that?
JASON. Oh, you won't believe it if I tell you. It's garlic. *(He hands the bottle to her. She takes it and immediately drops it as if she were burned.)* Hon?
BARBARA. I...I'm so sorry. I suppose I am still a bit weak. *(She looks at the bottle.)* Maybe you better pick it up.
JASON. Sure, hon. *(He picks up the garlic.)*

(HILDA enters carrying a large book, followed by LINDA, who is carrying a pot of flowers.)

HILDA. Okay, let's get started. *(She stops suddenly, causing LINDA to collide with her. She quickly throws the book on the couch.)*
JASON. Barbara's all right. See? We won't be needing...
HILDA *(quickly)*. You mean you won't be trying my...my recipe?
BARBARA *(eyes HILDA)*. Recipe? *(She moves away from the group.)*
LINDA. Barbara? What's wrong, dear?
JASON. She's still a bit woozy.

HILDA *(moves to her)*. Yes, that's it, I'm sure. *(She puts on a false amiability.)* Is there something wrong, Barbara?

BARBARA. No. Nothing, I'm sure. What're you doing here?

HILDA. Oh, your mother bought that old frame from me. Silly old piece of junk, isn't it? *(She moves back to LINDA.)* Well, we got to talking and they invited me over for dinner.

JASON. Invited?

HILDA. I have a wonderful recipe which I told Linda about and she simply had to have me over to fix it.

BARBARA. A recipe? With garlic. What dish are you preparing?

HILDA. Pizza!

JASON. What?!

HILDA. Yes. And while I was here, I noticed how...*(She sees the pot LINDA is holding.)*...how sick this plant was so we were planning on repotting it. *(She pulls the flowers out of the pot in one swift move.)* Dear, would you put these in the kitchen sink until we can prepare the pot? *(She hands the flowers to BARBARA.)*

BARBARA. What? Oh, of course. I'll see to it right away. *(She takes the flowers and looks around.)*

LINDA. The kitchen, Barbara. *(She points to the door.)* In there?

BARBARA. Yes...Mother. *(She smiles weakly and exits into the kitchen.)*

JASON. See? She's just fine, she...

HILDA. That's not her, that's the witch!

JASON. You're not still going on...

LINDA. Jay! She didn't even know where the kitchen was.

JASON. She's still a bit woozy, like I said.

HILDA. I knew you wouldn't believe me. That's why I had her take that bunch of flowers. Call her back.

JASON. What?

HILDA. Call her back and tell her to bring the flowers with her.

JASON. Oh, this is just...

LINDA. Do it! Oh! *(She yells.)* Barbara, we've changed our minds about the flowers. You better bring them back, dear.

JASON. What's this going to prove?

HILDA. Wait.

(BARBARA re-enters carrying the flowers. Now, however, the once fresh buds are dead and withered.)

BARBARA. Here you are. *(She hands the flower corpses to LINDA. JASON and LINDA stare at the flowers.)*

HILDA. Well, they were in worse shape than I first thought. *(She glares at LINDA.)* Maybe we better be getting ready for dinner.

LINDA. Huh? *(She snaps out of it.)* Oh, yeah. *(To BARBARA.)* Barbara, why don't you go freshen up and then we'll have dinner.

BARBARA. Yes. Yes, that is a good idea...Mother. *(She smiles and moves slowly up the stairs. She stops and looks back. The group smiles back at her. BARBARA exits.)*

JASON. How did those flowers...?

HILDA. Because everything she touches dies. You see now? That is *not* your daughter!

JASON. Oh my God!

LINDA. Now what?

HILDA. We don't have much time. *(She picks up the book from the couch and begins thumbing through the pages.)* Take the dirt from the flower pot and throw some in the mixing bowl. *(LINDA moves the pot to the coffee table next to the bowl. She pours dirt from the pot into the bowl.)*

LINDA. How much?

HILDA. Doesn't matter. Where's the garlic?

JASON. Huh? Oh, here. *(He hands the bottle to HILDA.)*

HILDA. Right. *(She opens the bottle and tips a bit of garlic into the bowl.)* Now. Something freshly killed.

LINDA. What?

JASON. Oh, that was the other ingredient.

LINDA. Where are we going to get something freshly killed?

HILDA. It can be anything. Quickly!

JASON. We got some Colonel Sanders chicken in the fridge.

LINDA. Jason!

JASON. I'm trying to think!

HILDA. Wait. *(She picks up one of the flowers.)* Maybe Elzbeth gave us our needed ingredient. *(She takes a few petals off the flower and gently places them in the bowl.)*

JASON *(after a beat)*. Nothing's happening.

HILDA. I brought the rest. *(She takes a pouch out of a pocket.)*

JASON. What's in there?

HILDA. You don't want to know. *(She starts to hand the pouch to JASON but instead gives it to LINDA.)* You.

LINDA. What do I do?

HILDA. When I nod to you, just pour the bag into the bowl.

LINDA. I don't understand. Didn't she recognize you as her granddaughter?

HILDA. Of course she did. The trick was I had to convince her that I *didn't* recognize her. It bought us a little time but we better hurry. Get on your knees.

JASON. Oh, you can't be serious.

LINDA. Jay! *(LINDA and JASON each kneel on opposite sides of the coffee table.)*

HILDA *(finds her place in the book)*. Ah, here it is. Place the frame next to the bowl. I don't know how strong this potion is going to be.

JASON. Right. *(He places the frame near the bowl.)*

HILDA. Oh yes. Don't be afraid.

JASON. I hate it when they start like that.

LINDA. What's going to happen?

HILDA. Beats heck out of me.

JASON. You don't inspire us, you know.

HILDA. What, you think I do this everyday? Now, quiet. *(To LINDA.)* And get the pouch ready. *(LINDA holds the pouch near the bowl.)* Now. *(She reads.)* "From the other side of the light, from the other side of the grave, from the spirits of the netherworld, bring us together here in unison, endeavor through the realm and seek to replace and replenish the power!" *(A loud thunderclap.)*

JASON. What the...!

HILDA *(louder)*. "Since time began, since the raven first flew, since the black wing of the bat cast its shadow over the fresh-dug earth, bring forth that manifest of what once was and tonight shall be again!" *(A louder thunderclap, with continuous thunder following.)* "Move closer to the realm and grant us the power. Cross over and replace what once was! Take away that spirit of evil and return it to its vessel! By virtue of the wolf bane, by the hidden secrets of its..." *(She stops.)*

LINDA. What? Why did you stop?

HILDA *(leans over and shows LINDA the book)*. What's that word?

JASON. Oh my...!

LINDA. Properties.

HILDA. Thank you. "...properties, allow us to undo that which began in evil and continues through the innocent.

Return the evil spirit now, as I command you!" *(A woman's scream is heard offstage.)*

JASON. Barbara! *(He starts to rise.)*

HILDA. Stay! Do not move. Pay no attention to anything you hear!

JASON. But...

HILDA. Do as I say! *(She continues.)* "That price that purchased her return shall be forfeit, shall return null what began corrupt into this world. Return it now!" *(She picks up the frame.)* "I command it to be replaced, restored back to its place. I command it...NOW!" *(She nods and LINDA pours in the powder. A very loud thunderclap along with another scream from offstage. The very power of the noise dims the lights and causes HILDA to drop the frame to the floor. Then, the scream dies away slowly. The lights return to normal and HILDA sinks to her knees. There is a slight, uneasy pause.)*

JASON. Well?

HILDA *(nods and exhales deeply).* It's done.

LINDA. It is? Are you sure? *(HILDA reaches down and holds up the frame. She turns it around to reveal Barbara's picture is once again in place.)*

JASON *(believing it).* I don't believe it.

LINDA. It's her picture! It's Barbara's picture. *(She takes the frame and rises.)* She's back!

HILDA. Only because we acted in time. *(She and JASON get to their feet. She quickly moves to LINDA and takes the frame. She gently removes Barbara's picture and hands it to LINDA.)* I shudder to think what would've happened if I hadn't gotten here when I did.

LINDA *(crosses to the stairs).* Barbara? Barbara, are you all right? *(A brief pause.)*

BARBARA *(from offstage).* Mom? Is...is that you?

LINDA. Yes, hon. We're downstairs.
BARBARA. Dad?
JASON. Right here, shug.
HILDA. Now, may I have my frame?
LINDA. Yes, of course! Take that...that thing far away from here!
JASON. And guard it well.
HILDA. I will. It's a lifetime job. You see how it is. *(She moves to the front door.)*
LINDA. I don't know how to thank you.
JASON. Well, she can send us our check back.
HILDA *(smiles)*. Once a lawyer, always a lawyer. Oh. Happy Halloween. *(She smiles weakly and exits. JASON crosses over and re-lights the jack-o'lantern.)*
LINDA. What're you doing?
JASON. Trying to get things back to normal.
LINDA. I just hope that we can always be sure of what's normal. Before today...
JASON. Today never happened. There's no way we can ever fully understand it. And certainly no way we will ever be able to talk of it.
LINDA. I guess you're right. *(She crosses to JASON.)* I wonder if she knows.
JASON. Barbara? *(LINDA nods.)* We'll let her bring it up. Otherwise...
LINDA. Act normal, I know. *(She looks into the fireplace.)* I'm just glad it's all over. And that...that "whatever" is back in the frame. *(JASON looks up slowly and over at LINDA meaningfully.)*
JASON. Yes. The spirit is...gone from Barbara.
LINDA. And back in the frame, I...Wait. How do we know it's back in the...*(She turns quickly to see JASON moving slowly up behind her.)* What're you...?

JASON. What?

LINDA *(suddenly frantic)*. Jason!

JASON *(smiles and relaxes)*. Hon? It's me. Jason Muir, married to Linda Muir, used to be Parker. We live in this three bedroom house with...*(LINDA hugs him suddenly.)*

LINDA. Sorry. I don't know what I was...

JASON. I know, dear. Like you said, what's normal?

LINDA *(calls out)*. Barbara?

JASON. I think tonight we'll just hand out the treats and leave off the ghost stories.

LINDA. Had enough...finally?

JASON. Just happy to have the three of us back together.

LINDA. Barbara!

(Quickly coming down the stairs, not BARBARA, but a very old, very wrinkled WITCH.)

JASON. Bar—*(He and LINDA turn and see the WITCH.)* No! NOOO! *(LINDA screams and falls to her knees.)*

WITCH. Yeeeesss. Just the three of us. *(She crosses to the jack-o'lantern.)* It's so good to be back. (Suddenly the eerie music begins loudly and the lights black out. Only the grinning jack-o'lantern is seen. Slowly, the WITCH picks up the pumpkin, the light shining through its top illuminates her face. She turns to the audience, moves toward them and stops. Then, she cackles and speaks.) Boo! *(She blows out the jack-o'lantern and...)*

BLACKOUT
END OF PLAY

DIRECTOR'S NOTES